Albert Pujols
A Baseball Star Who Cares

Jeff C. Young

Enslow Elementary
an imprint of

Enslow Publishers, Inc.
40 Industrial Road
Box 398
Berkeley Heights, NJ 07922
USA

http://www.enslow.com

Enlsow Elementary, an imprint of Enslow Publishers, Inc.

Enslow Elementary® is a registered trademark of Enslow Publishers, Inc.

Library of Congress Cataloging-in-Publication Data

Young, Jeff C., 1948–
  Albert Pujols : a baseball star who cares / Jeff C. Young.
     p. cm. — (Sports stars who care)
  Includes bibliographical references and index.
  Summary: "Learn about all-star first baseman Albert Pujols, and how he got to where he is now in this sports biography. He is one of baseball's best players ever, but off of the field, he has become a sports star who really does care"--Provided by publisher.
  ISBN 978-0-7660-4228-5
  1. Pujols, Albert, 1980– —Juvenile literature. 2. Baseball players—United States—Biography—Juvenile literature. I. Title.
  GV865.P85Y68 2013
  796.357092—dc23
  [B]
                          2012039418

Future Editions:
Paperback ISBN: 978-1-4644-0399-6
EPUB ISBN: 978-1-4645-1219-3
Single-User PDF ISBN: 978-1-4646-1219-0
Multi-User PDF ISBN: 978-0-7660-5851-4

052013 Lake Book Manufacturing, Inc., Melrose Park, IL

10 9 8 7 6 5 4 3 2 1

Printed in the United States of America

To Our Readers:
We have done our best to make sure all Internet addresses in this book were active and appropriate when we went to press. However, the author and the Publisher have no control over, and assume no liability for, the material available on those Internet sites or on other Web sites they may link to. Any comments or suggestions can be sent by e-mail to comments@enslow.com or to the address on the back cover.

✪ Enslow Publishers, Inc., is committed to printing our books on recycled paper. The paper in every book contains 10% to 30% post-consumer waste (PCW). The cover board on the outside of each book contains 100% PCW. Our goal is to do our part to help young people and the environment too!

Photo Credits: AP Images/Charlie Riedel, p. 9; AP Images/Chris Carlson, pp. 4, 14; AP Images/David J. Phillip, pp. 34, 35; AP Images/Eric Gay, p. 10; AP Images/Four Seam Images/Larry Goren, pp. 1, 36; AP Images/James A. Finley, p. 16; AP Images/Jeff Roberson, pp. 11, 18, 39; AP Images/*St. Louis Post-Dispatch*/Huy Mach, p. 42; AP Images/Tom DiPace, p. 28; AP Images/Tom Gannam, pp. 21, 23, 24, 26, 32, 41; AP Images/Winslow Townson, p. 29.

Cover Illustration: AP Images/Four Seam Images/Larry Goren

Contents

Introduction

Since becoming a major-league player in 2001, Albert Pujols has become one of the game's most feared and respected hitters. Many sportswriters and commentators have called him a natural because he often makes hitting a baseball look easy.

Even though his success has come quickly, Pujols has never taken it for granted. He's maintained a demanding year-round training regimen. He still spends many hours in batting cages practicing and perfecting his swing and timing. When he's off the field, he spends additional hours studying videos of opposing pitchers.

Although he's noted for his hitting, Pujols is also an excellent fielder who's won two Gold Glove Awards. He's also a smart base runner who seldom makes a mistake on the base paths.

Simply calling Pujols a great baseball player doesn't completely describe him. Being a good husband, father, and role model is as important to him as being a good player and teammate.

"It's part of my responsibility to play the game the right way and be an example to kids who look up to me, just like when I was a little boy and looked up to big league players," Pujols said. "I know how many kids out there want to be like Albert Pujols."

Being a role model and setting a good example isn't something that Pujols merely talks about. In 2005, Pujols and his wife, Deidre, established the Pujols Family Foundation. The foundation works to improve the quality of life for children with Down syndrome. It's something they care deeply about because their oldest daughter, Isabella, has Down syndrome.

Their foundation also provides funds for educational opportunities and medical services for needy children in the Dominican Republic, their native country.

Hitting home runs was nothing new for Albert Pujols. In 11 major-league seasons with the St. Louis Cardinals, he had done it 445 times. But a spectacular display of power hitting in Game 3 of the 2011 World Series forever linked his name with two Hall of Fame players and World Series heroes:

Chapter 1

A Career Moment

Babe Ruth and Reggie Jackson. On that night, Pujols became only the third player to hit three home runs in a World Series game.

Ruth did it twice as a New York Yankee against the Cardinals in 1926 and 1928. Jackson also did it as a Yankee in 1977. His three consecutive homers on three consecutive pitches in Game 7 gave the Yankees a World Series championship against the Los Angeles Dodgers.

Pujols's first home run came in the top of the sixth inning with two men on and St. Louis leading 8–6. Texas Rangers pitcher Alexi Ogando tried to blaze a 96 mile-per-hour fastball past Pujols. For an ordinary batter, it would have been hard to hit. The pitch was shoulder high and on the inner half of the plate. Pujols smashed it into the second deck of left field. The ball traveled an estimated 432 feet.

"It's hard to hit a ball that far," said Pujols's teammate, Matt Holliday, "let alone off of a guy throwing 96, letter-high. Not a lot of guys, if any, can do that."

An inning later, Pujols swatted his second home run. It was on a first-pitch fastball from Mike Gonzalez. The two-run shot traveled 424 feet before landing into the seats in the deep left-center field section of Rangers Ballpark. Along with being his second home run, it was Pujols's fourth hit in four innings. That made him the first player to get four hits in four consecutive innings (fourth, fifth, sixth, and seventh) in a World Series game.

Despite having hit so many home runs, Pujols was still in awe of this massive shot he hit off of Alexi Ogando.

With the Cardinals leading 14–6 in the ninth inning, Pujols thought about asking his manager, Tony LaRussa, to take him out of the game. He didn't. That gave Pujols one final trip to the plate. He got it when the Cardinals were down to their last out.

On a 2–2 count, Pujols fouled off a pitch from Darren Oliver that came very close to being an out.

Albert Pujols will do whatever it takes to win. He is a team player that wants to make others around him succeed.

The foul ball fell just beyond the reach of Rangers first baseman Michael Young. Holliday was standing in the on-deck circle. He saw that Pujols still looked relaxed and confident.

"I looked at him," Holliday said, "and he kind of smiled like that could have been the third one. So he did it—on the next pitch."

That next pitch was an 89 mile-per-hour sinker that Pujols hit into the lower deck of the left field seats. Pujols ended the game going 5-for-6 and tying two other World Series records. He became the second player to get five hits in a World Series game. And he was just the third player to get six RBI in a World Series game. He also set a new World Series record by getting 14 total bases (three home runs and two singles) in a game.

Pujols was flattered to be compared with two of the game's best sluggers. But he added that helping his team win was more important than setting records.

"Those guys are great players, and to do it at that level and on this stage is amazing," he said. "But at the same time, I didn't walk into the ballpark today thinking that I was going to have a night like this. I walked to the ballpark with the attitude that I have every day, to help this ball club to win, and I was able to do that."

A lbert Pujols was born January 16, 1980 in Santo Domingo, the capital city of the Dominican Republic. The Dominican Republic is a small country which makes up the eastern two-thirds of the Caribbean island of Hispaniola. The country

Chapter 2

The Early Years

Albert enjoys representing the Dominican Republic in the World Baseball Classic. This is him during the 2006 classic.

of Haiti makes up the other third. Albert was the youngest of twelve children. His parents divorced when he was very young, so he was raised by his father, Bienvenido, and his grandmother, America.

Bienvenido pitched in the minor leagues in the Dominican Republic. Albert watched his father play as often as he could, and he quickly developed a love of baseball. Albert loved and admired his father, but Bienvenido had a serious drinking problem. There were times when Albert had to help his father get home after a game.

Albert and the neighborhood boys that he played baseball with were too poor to buy baseball equipment for their pickup games. They used tree branches for bats, cardboard milk cartons for gloves, and rolled up socks or limes for baseballs.

When Albert was in his early teens, he received some invitations to baseball camps sponsored by major-league teams. The best players would get offers from major-league teams. At that time, Albert wasn't a standout player. He didn't get any offers, but he didn't let that discourage him. He never stopped believing that someday he would be a major-league player.

The Pujols family immigrated to the United Sates when Albert was sixteen. They moved to New York City, but they only stayed there for about a month. America felt that the part of the city where they lived wasn't a safe place for the family. They packed up and

Albert and his wife, Deidre, arrive for a press conference.

moved to Independence, Missouri. Several of Albert's aunts and uncles were working there as school bus drivers.

Albert enrolled at Fort Osage High School as a sophomore. School was hard for him. He had to take daily one-on-one lessons to learn English. The language barrier also gave Albert some trouble when he played high school baseball. At first, he had some trouble understanding some of the rules.

When Albert first met David Fry, the Fort Osage baseball coach, he had to use an interpreter to speak to him. The interpreter told Fry that Albert wanted to play baseball. Coach Fry would later say: "The baseball gods were smiling on me that day."

Albert quickly impressed his coach with his exceptional talent and his commitment to improving his skills. "He was so driven to succeed, always stayed behind to take extra batting practice or ground balls," Fry said.

One of the most memorable moments of Albert's high school career was a towering home run against Liberty High School. The ball traveled over 400 feet, and landed on an air conditioning unit atop a nearby building.

In his first season of high school baseball, Albert batted over .500 with 11 home runs. His hitting helped Fort Osage to go 21–7 and win a state championship.

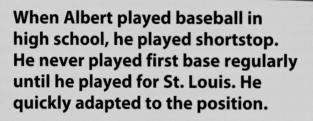

When Albert played baseball in high school, he played shortstop. He never played first base regularly until he played for St. Louis. He quickly adapted to the position.

Albert's home run production declined during his junior year because opposing pitchers began walking him. He drew 55 walks in only 88 at bats. Still, he managed to hit eight home runs, and he received all-state honors for the second straight year. By then, he was attracting the attention of major-league scouts.

Some of those scouts advised Albert to graduate from high school early and skip his senior season of high school baseball. Albert followed their advice and enrolled in some extra classes. He graduated from Fort Osage High School in January 1998.

While taking the extra classes, Albert played in a game with other high school all-stars from the Kansas City area. Marty Kilgore, the baseball coach at Maple Woods Community College, saw Albert play and recruited him for the school's baseball team. College baseball became the next step to Albert becoming a major-league player.

Pujols had no trouble making the adjustment from high school to college baseball. In his first game for Maple Woods Community College, he quickly impressed everyone with both his hitting and his fielding. He hit a grand slam home run, and made an unassisted triple

Chapter 3

College and Minor Leagues

The St. Louis Cardinals knew Albert would end up making the big leagues. But no one could have imagined the impact he would have.

play while playing shortstop. Pujols finished his freshman year of college baseball with 22 home runs, 80 RBI, and a .461 batting average.

In spite of that spectacular season, Pujols was overlooked in the early rounds of the Major League Draft. There were rumors that he was out of shape. Since he was born in the Dominican Republic, there were also questions about when he was born. When the 1999 Major League Draft was held, Pujols became the 13th round pick of the St. Louis Cardinals. That made him the 402nd player chosen.

"He was devastated," recalled Russ Meyer, who had scouted Pujols for the Kansas City Royals. "He kept saying, 'I know I'm better than that.'"

The Cardinals offered Pujols a $10,000 bonus, but he didn't think that was enough. He turned down their offer and spent the summer of 1999 playing for the Hays Larks of the Jayhawk League. The league was made up of other college players looking to improve their skills. Pujols led the Larks in home runs and batting. That impressed the Cardinals enough to raise their bonus to $60,000. This time, he accepted their offer.

There are three levels of minor-league baseball: A, AA, and AAA. Most players will play at all three levels before they make it to the major leagues. Sometimes an exceptional player will go directly from high school or college baseball to the major leagues, but that rarely happens.

Pujols began his minor-league career with the Cardinals Potomac team in the Carolina League. After batting .284 in 21 games, he was promoted to the Cardinals Class A Peoria team in the Midwestern

League. In 124 games for Peoria, Pujols batted .324 with 17 home runs and 84 RBI. He was voted Most Valuable Player (MVP) of the Midwestern League, and was promoted to the Cardinals AAA team, the Memphis Redbirds, of the Pacific Coast League (PCL).

It was late in the season when Pujols was called up to Memphis, so he only appeared in three regular season games. However, the Redbirds had advanced to the PCL World Series. Pujols was named the series MVP after batting .367 with two home runs and five RBI in seven games. It was a dazzling finish to his

Albert Pujols is all smiles after winning the NL MVP Award.

first season in the minor leagues.

In just one year, Pujols had advanced from the lowest to the highest level of minor-league baseball. He skipped the AA level, and at the age of twenty he was only one level away from playing in the major leagues. Pujols was already looking forward to the Cardinals 2001 spring training camp. It was a chance to prove that he was better than most, if not all, of the 401 players who were chosen ahead of him.

When Pujols reported to the Cardinals spring training camp in 2001, he was one of the few people who believed that he could make the major-league club. St. Louis' manager, Tony LaRussa, had planned on Pujols spending some more time in the minor leagues.

Chapter 4

Early Pro Career

Hall-of-Fame broadcaster Jack Buck interviews Albert before one of Pujols's first major-league games in 2001.

That changed when Bobby Bonilla, one of the Cardinals starting outfielders, suffered a hamstring injury before opening day. That opened up a spot on the roster for Pujols. On Opening Day, he was in the lineup as the Cardinals left fielder.

Pujols quickly showed that he was ready for the major leagues. In his first month, he won the National League Rookie of the Month Award by batting .370

and hitting eight home runs in April. That was just the start of an incredible rookie season.

In 161 games, he batted .329 with 37 home runs and 130 RBI. Pujols was unanimously named the National League Rookie of the Year. After winning the award, he credited hard work and his manager's confidence in him for his outstanding season.

"If you work hard every day, you always reach your goal," Pujols said. "Tony [LaRussa] put that trust in me and gave me the opportunity to prove myself and make the team."

If there were some skeptics who thought that Pujols would be a one-season wonder, he proved them wrong in 2002. His second season in the major leagues was as impressive as his first. Pujols batted .314 while clubbing 34 home runs with 127 RBI. That made him the first player in major-league history to hit over 30 home runs and have over 100 RBI in his first two seasons.

In 2003, Pujols led the National League in four offensive categories: batting (.359), runs scored (137), hits (212), and doubles (51). Yet his hitting heroics were not enough to get the Cardinals into postseason play.

Before the start of the 2004 season, St. Louis signed Pujols to a seven-year, $100 million contract extension. He showed the club it was a smart investment by leading the Cardinals to the World Series. Pujols hit for a high average (.331) while leading the National

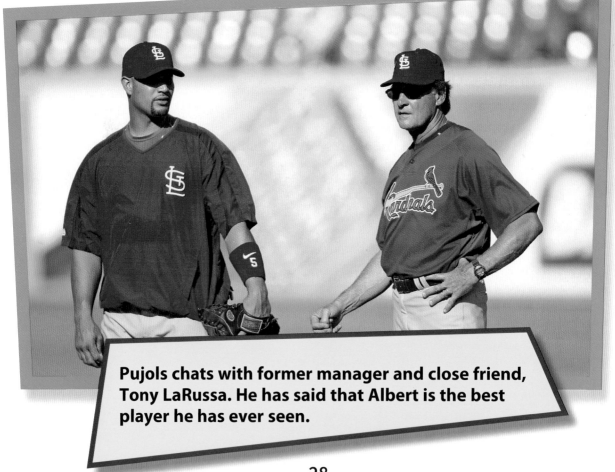

Pujols chats with former manager and close friend, Tony LaRussa. He has said that Albert is the best player he has ever seen.

Pujols and former Red Sox outfielder Manny Ramirez talk before the first game of the 2004 World Series.

League in runs scored (133) for the second straight year. He was also among the National League leaders in home runs (46) and RBI (123).

After St. Louis won the National League's Central Division, Pujols batted .333 to lead his team past the Los Angeles Dodgers in the National League Division Series (NLDS). Then he batted .500 against the Houston Astros in the National League Championship Series (NLCS). Pujols was named MVP (Most Valuable Player) of the NLCS, and the Cardinals advanced to face the Boston Red Sox in the World Series.

Even though he batted .333 in the World Series, that didn't prevent the Cardinals from losing to the Red Sox in a four game sweep.

After four seasons in the major leagues, Pujols had earned a reputation as one of the game's most feared hitters. During that time, he averaged 40 home runs, 126 RBI, and 125 runs scored per season. He had also been a Rookie of the Year, National League batting champion, and three-time All-Star. About the only thing missing was a World Series championship.

In 2005 the Cardinals won the National League Central Division for the second year in a row. Once again, Pujols played a major role in the team's continuing success. For the fifth consecutive season, he batted over .300 while hitting over 30 home runs, scoring over 100 runs, and

Chapter 5

Recent Pro Career

totaling over 100 RBI. That outstanding performance earned him his first National League Most Valuable Player Award.

Pujols also continued to do very well in postseason play. In the NLDS, he led the Cardinals to a three game sweep of the San Diego Padres while batting .556. Against the Houston Astros in the NLCS, Pujols batted. 304, but St. Louis lost the series, four games to two.

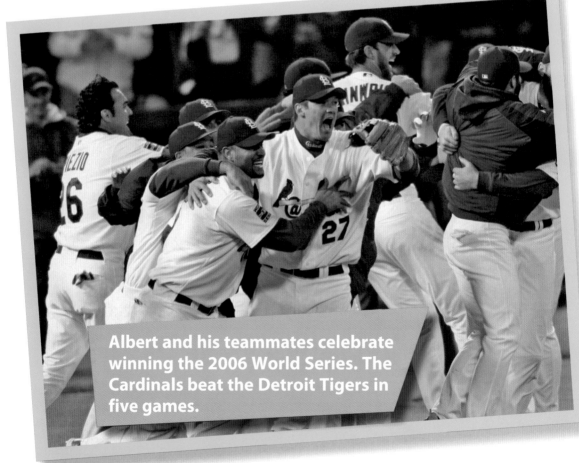

Albert and his teammates celebrate winning the 2006 World Series. The Cardinals beat the Detroit Tigers in five games.

The next season, the Cardinals won their first World Series in twenty-four years. They defeated the Detroit Tigers, four games to one. Pujols batted over .300 in both the NLDS and NLCS, but he only batted .200 with one home run and two RBI in the World Series. Still, he was delighted to be adding a 2006 World Series ring to his trophy case.

"Now I can say that I have a World Series ring in my trophy case," Pujols said. "And that's what you play for. It doesn't matter how much money you make or what kind of numbers you put up in the big leagues. If you walk out of this game and you don't have a ring, you haven't accomplished everything."

While Pujols was winning major awards for his play, he was being honored for helping and inspiring others through the work of the Pujols Family Foundation. In November 2006 he received the Marvin Miller Man of the Year Award from the MLB Players Association. The award is given every year to the MLB player whose on-field performance and off-the-field contributions to his community inspire others to achieve more.

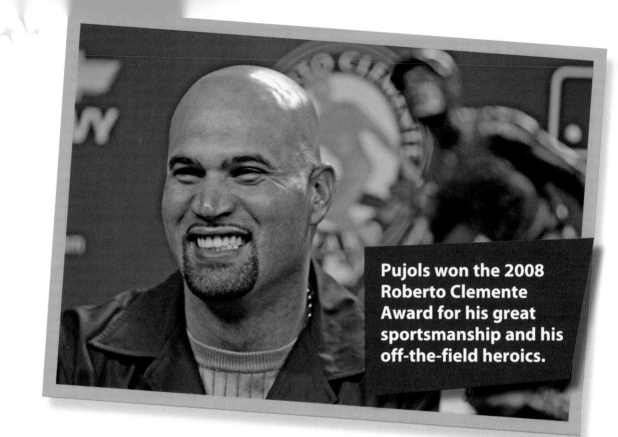

Pujols won the 2008 Roberto Clemente Award for his great sportsmanship and his off-the-field heroics.

Later, in 2008, Pujols received the Roberto Clemente Award. That award is given to the MLB player who best exemplifies the game of baseball, sportsmanship, community involvement, and contributions to his team.

After winning back-to-back NL MVP Awards in 2008 and 2009, Pujols was named the MLB Player of the Decade by both *The Sporting News* and *Sports Illustrated*. In 2010 he had his tenth consecutive season of batting over .300 with over 30 home runs and 100 RBI.

The 2011 season could be considered a slightly below average year for Pujols. A wrist injury caused him to miss 15 games. For the first time in his major league career, Pujols batted below .300 and had less than 100 RBI. Still, he came very close to reaching those numbers. He batted .299 and had 99 RBI.

Once again, Pujols did well in the postseason competition. He led the Cardinals into the World

Pujols and the Cardinals celebrate winning the 2011 World Series!

After weeks of talking with a few teams, Pujols signed a huge contract with the Los Angeles Angels of Anaheim.

Series by batting .350 in the NLDS and .478 in the NLCS. Although he only hit .240 in the World Series, Pujols hit three home runs in Game 3. He added another World Series ring to his trophy case as the Cardinals beat the Texas Rangers, four games to three.

After the 2011 World Series, Pujols became a free agent. He had said that he wanted to stay in St. Louis, but he wanted a long-term contract. The Cardinals offered him a five-year deal, but the Los Angeles Angels of Anaheim were able to offer him what he wanted. In January 2012, Pujols signed a ten-year contract with the Angels that will pay him around $254 million.

After switching to a new team and a new league, Pujols got off to a slow start in 2012. By mid-May, he was batting below .200. He was briefly benched before he began hitting again. By late June he had raised his batting average to over .250. Pujols finished the season with a .285 average, 30 home runs, and 100 RBI. If he plays another ten years, it is likely that he will be among the all-time leaders in home runs, RBI, and runs scored.

No matter how long he plays, Pujols will always strive to be the best player he can be, and continue to help and inspire others through the work of the Pujols Family Foundation.

In 2005, Pujols and his wife, Deidre, wanted to give back to their community. They established the Pujols Family Foundation. The foundation is a nonprofit organization which works to support and aid people with Down syndrome. The foundation also supports people with other challenges, disabilities,

Chapter 6

Charitable Contributions

Albert speaks during a benefit for the Pujols Family Foundation.

and life-threatening illnesses. It also works to aid the needy in the Dominican Republic by providing educational opportunities and medical care.

Down syndrome is a disorder caused by an abnormal number of chromosomes. Chromosomes are the parts of a cell which house tiny structures called genes. Genes determine hereditary traits. People with Down syndrome have forty-seven genes instead of the usual forty-six (or twenty-three pairs). A person with Down syndrome will have severe to mild mental retardation.

Down syndrome also causes various birth defects, such as problems with hearing, vision, and the heart. Many children with Down syndrome are small for their age and have delayed physical and mental development. The Pujols' oldest child, Isabella, was born with Down syndrome.

Since its founding, the Pujols Family Foundation has raised millions of dollars through auctions and an annual golf tournament. The foundation has generously donated funds to the Down Syndrome Association of Greater St. Louis. Those funds have

Albert's children, Albert, Jr., and Isabella, are seen with their dad changing the 'Games Remaining' number at Busch Stadium.

Albert meets with former Cardinals teammates Matt Holliday and Jason Motte at the 2012 Matt Holliday Celebrity Golf Classic. Proceeds benefitted the Pujols Family Foundation.

enabled the association to open an office and hire the staff to run it. In 2009, the foundation raised $1.3 million in contributions and grants.

Money raised by the foundation has established family events to enrich the lives of children with Down syndrome. Those events include father-son fishing tournaments, mother-daughter bowling tournaments, cooking classes, and classes in self-defense and conflict resolution. The foundation also hosts an annual prom for teenagers with Down syndrome.

Funds raised by the foundation have also financed sending a team of doctors and dentists to the Dominican Republic to provide medical care and dental services to needy Dominicans. The foundation has also sent school supplies, shoes, and other needed goods to the Orfanato Ninos de Cristo orphanage in Santo Domingo.

Even though the Pujols family has left St. Louis, the good work and deeds of the foundation will continue on an even larger scale. They are currently expanding to open offices in Kansas City, Nashville, and Southern California. That shows that Albert Pujols truly is a sports star who cares.

Year	Team	G	AB	R	H	2B	3B	HR	RBI	SB	AVG
2001	Cards	161	590	112	194	47	4	37	130	1	.329
2002	Cards	157	590	118	185	40	2	34	127	2	.341
2003	Cards	157	591	137	212	51	1	43	124	5	.359
2004	Cards	154	592	133	196	51	2	46	123	5	.331
2005	Cards	161	591	129	195	38	2	41	117	16	.330
2006	Cards	143	535	119	177	33	1	49	137	7	.331
2007	Cards	158	565	99	185	38	1	32	103	2	.327
2008	Cards	148	524	100	187	44	0	37	116	7	.357
2009	Cards	160	568	124	186	45	1	47	135	16	.327
2010	Cards	159	587	115	183	39	1	42	118	14	.312
2011	Cards	147	579	105	173	29	0	37	99	9	.299
2012	Angels	154	607	85	173	50	0	30	105	8	.285
	TOTALS	1,859	6,919	1,376	2,246	505	15	475	1,434	92	.325

G = Games   2B = Doubles   SB = Stolen Bases
AB = At Bats   3B = Triples   AVG = Batting Average
R = Runs   HR = Home Runs
H = Hits   RBI = Runs Batted In

Where to Write

ALBERT PUJOLS
c/o LOS ANGELES ANGELS OF ANAHEIM
2000 East Gene Autry Way
Anaheim, CA 92806.

abnormal—Not normal or average.

commentator—A person who discusses or describes events on radio or television.

consecutive—Following in order with no gaps.

decade—A period of ten years.

Down syndrome—A condition characterized by moderate to severe mental retardation.

devastated—Deeply disappointed.

exemplify—To show by example.

free agent—A player who is free to sign a contract with any team that he chooses.

hamstring—Any of several muscles at the back of the thigh or tendons at the back of the knee.

hereditary—Characteristics passed on from parents to their children.

manager—The head coach of a baseball team.

MLB—Major League Baseball; the highest level of professional baseball.

RBI—Runs batted in.

regimen—A regularly followed course of treatment or training.

reputation—The overall quality or character as seen or judged by people in general.

résumé—A short account of someone's career accomplishments, awards and achievements.

sinker—A pitch with a sharp downward curve as it reaches that plate.

skeptics—People with a doubting attitude.

standout—A person who is clearly superior to others.

unanimously—Totally in agreement.

Read More

Books

Gaspar, Joe. *Albert Pujols: Amazing Hitter.* New York: PowerKids Press, 2011.

Mattern, Joanne. *Albert Pujols: Baseball Superstar.* Mankato, Minn.: Capstone Press, 2012.

Needham, Tom. *Albert Pujols: MVP On And Off The Field.* Berkeley Heights, N.J.: Enslow Publishers, Inc., 2008.

Rodriquez, Tania. *Albert Pujols.* Broomall, Pa.: Mason Crest Publishers, 2013.

Internet Addresses

www.baseball-almanac.com

www.baseball-reference.com

www.losangeles.angels.mlb.com

www.pujolsfamilyfoundation.org

Index